# CONTENTS

# cookie

## WHEAT FLOUR

All the recipes in this book call for soft wheat flour, which has less gluten and bakes to crumblier cookies. Sift flour before using and add one half or one third of flour at a time when making dough. Use hard wheat flour for dusting a board and a rolling pin to prevent dough from sticking.

## EGGS

Eggs play important roles as butter and flour do in making cookies. Always buy fresh eggs in good quality and use them up for a short time. If the weight of egg is indicated in the recipe, beat egg lightly and weigh the required amount. Depending on the amount of eggs used, the baked cookies taste different. Always use the indicated amount of eggs.

## BUTTER

There are Salt butter and Sweet butter. Sweet butter has delicate flavor but salt butter keeps longer. Use whichever you like except for making buttercream which requires sweet butter. Have butter at room temperature (about 24°C) before you use. Beat butter with a wire whisk until light and fluffy, then mix with other ingredients. If you melt butter instead, baked cookies will not be crispy.

## SUGAR

Sugar is used for sweetening and browning cookies. Use refined white sugar which is easily dissolved and can be mixed well into eggs or butter. Granulated sugar is also used for making cakes and cookies. This contains less moisture and is sometimes used for sprinkling over baked cookies. Confectioners' sugar is a finer grind of granulated sugar and is added 3% of cornstarch to prevent from lumping. This is mostly used for icing.

## BAKING POWDER & BAKING SODA

Baking Powder consists of carbon acid and alkaline material. When mixed with water and heated, they form a gas called carbon dioxide which rises dough or batter. Too much use of baking powder will spoil the taste of cookies. Baking Soda has a leavening power twice as much as baking powder, so measure accurately as indicated. Sift baking powder with flour and dissolve baking soda in water.

## GROUND ALMONDS AND CORNSTARCH

Ground almonds is called "amande poudre" in French. This gives dough flavor and rich taste. You can make marzipan by mixing ground almonds and confectioners' sugar in the proportion of two to one and kneading with a little water or egg white. Cornstarch is made from corn and is powdery. It does not contain any gluten, so when mixed with water it does not become elastic.

## WHIPPING CREAM

This is skimmed from whole milk. Depending on the proportion of butterfat, it is called Heavy cream or Light cream, and the former is used for decorating cakes and the latter for coffee. When whipping heavy cream, make sure the bowl and whisk are free from grease and water. Place the bowl over ice water and beat. Ready-made whipped cream seasoned with sugar and flavor is available. Once opened the pack, it must be used. If kept open, it will spoil.

## CHOCOLATE & COCOA

Sift cocoa and flour together to make brown dough. Cocoa is also used for coloring icing. Chocolate is used for making cookies, decorating and coating. For coating cookies, use semisweet chocolate or coating chocolate which contains cocoa butter. When using sweetened chocolate squares for coating, you may add some melted butter for smooth surface.

## ICING AND FOOD COLOR

Icing makes cookies lovely, keeps and add flavor and helps from drying. It is also used for joining cookies. Use icing as it is or color as you like. There are many food colors available both in liquid and dry forms. You can make various colors by mixing a few colors.

## LIQUOR AND ESSENCE

Few drops of liquor is sometimes added to flavor whipped cream. Choose liquor in high quality and flavor. A collection of miniature bottles of rum, brandy, kirsch and liqueur is helpful. Various kinds of essence are also used for making cookies. The recipes in this book call for vanilla extract when adding to the unbaked food and vanilla oil to the dough to be baked. **When making cookies for Muslim friends, use only essence and don't use any liquor.**

## CANDIED FRUITS AND JAMS

Many kinds of candied and liquored fruits are available at stores. Orange peel, angelica, candied cherries, unsweetened cherries and canned blackberries are often used for decoration. Jam is used for glazing over baked cookies and for filling.

## NUTS

Nuts are used for making dough or decoration cookies. Blanch almonds or walnuts in hot water to remove inner skin. Toast them in the low-heated oven. When you use raw slivered almonds, also toast in the oven. Shredded coconuts are available at food stores. Poppy seeds have special flavor and are used for sprinkling over baked cookies.

## DECORATION

Don't overcrowd with decoration. Silver dragées, in small and large sizes, are made of poppy seeds coated with sugar and tinted in silver. Marzipan or almond paste is also used for making shapes for decoration. It is available at cake-decoration supply stores. Flavor almond paste with liqueur or essence, color with food colors and form into desired shapes like handling clay.

## SPICES

Spices are used for adding flavor to cookies. Ground cinnamon is often used for cookies, cakes and desserts. Clove is a dried bud of the clove tree and resembles a nail. Ground clove is used for cookies. Ground ginger and paprika are also used.

## DIAL SCALE, MEASURING CUP AND SPOONS

One of the most important things in making cookies is to measure necessary ingredients accurately. Use dial scales which can weigh from 1 g to 1 kg. Sift flour and any powdery ingredients before measuring if you use a measuring cup or spoons. When weight of egg is indicated in the recipe, weigh after lightly beaten. Measuring cup contains 200 c.c., 1 tablespoon (Ts) 15 c.c. and 1 teaspoon (ts) 5 c.c.

## SIFTER AND TEA STRAINER

Flour, sugar, cocoa and any powdered ingredients should be sifted before using in order to eliminate lumps and make them mix well with butter, eggs or other ingredients. Air is trapped into flour by sifting and baked cookies become light and crispy. Use a sifter as shown which has three layers of sieves. Tea strainer is used for sprinkling confectioners' sugar over cookies.

## MIXING BOWLS AND WIRE WHISK

Mixing bowls are necessary for mixing ingredients and beating eggs, butter or heavy cream. Prepare a set of three deep bowls with flat bottom in small, medium and large sizes made of stainless steel. Wire whisk is used for beating eggs, heavy cream or butter to incorporate air. 30 cm-long, stainless steel wire whisk with sturdy grip is recommended. The bigger the whisk is, the easier to handle for a beginner.

## WOODEN SPATULA AND RUBBER SCRAPER

Wooden spatula is used for mixing, stirring or folding ingredients when making cookies, custard cream or other sauces. Rubber scraper is helpful for scraping batter or cream from a bowl. When mixing flour with beaten egg or creamed butter, don't stir but fold like cutting dough.

## PASTRY CLOTH AND ROLLING PIN

For rolling out dough on a board, use a cotton pastry cloth to prevent dough from sticking and also for turning dough easily with the cloth. A big and heavy rolling pin with ball-bearling grips is advisable for forming a bigger and even shape. Roll from the center outwards giving same pressure to the right and left sides.

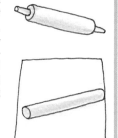

## COOKIE CUTTERS AND PETTY KNIFE

Cookie cutters are necessary for cutting out shapes from rolled dough. Various kinds of cutters made of plastic or stainless steel are available. Choose thin-edged cutters for cutting out neatly. Place the cutter at right angles and press in one breath. Wipe off dough sticked to the cutter each time it is used. When cutters are not available, use cardboard patterns and petty knife. A checker roller can mark all over rolled dough.

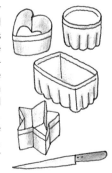

## WIRE RACK, PASTRY BAG AND METAL TUBES

Remove cookies from the oven immediately after they are baked onto wire racks with 2-3 cm legs to cool. Choose easy-to-handle pastry bags. Press the filled bag with your right hand and form a desired shape in one breath. You can make a bag for icing with wax paper (see page 11). Use the round metal tube, 1 cm in diameter for shaping cookies.

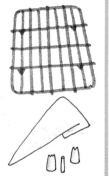

## BRUSHES AND BAMBOO STICK

Use flat or round brushes for wiping off extra flour from dough or glazing with diluted egg yolk, syrup, jam or icing. Choose brushes in good quality and wash and dry each time they are used. Bamboo stick is used for pricking, drawing rough designs or making small designs on the dough.

## ABOUT OVEN

To bake cookies properly, care must be taken to obtain the indicated temperature in the oven. The book indicates the temperature and baking time for each recipe, but you must check your oven and control it. When you bake small cookies, they are apt to brown quickly, so special care should be taken. In order to know your oven, place slices of bread all over a baking sheet, place the sheet in the middle of the oven and bake for a test. If the top of bread becomes browned faster than the bottom, place the sheet on the lower rack or place an empty sheet on the upper rack. If the bottom becomes browned faster, place an empty sheet on the lower rack or line the sheet with aluminum foil. When you cannot get even heating on the right or left side, turn the sheet before cookies are baked.

Preheat the oven 20 minutes or until the required temperature is reached before using. It takes time to obtain the indicated temperature in the oven. While making dough, preheat the oven.

## CLEANING

Always clean the oven and baking pans. Wash baking pans and dry thoroughly. Rub pans with salad-oiled towel. Grease them before you use to prevent cookies from sticking. Non-stick teflon-coated baking pans are available.

## EASY EQUIVALENTS

| Foods \ Measuring Spoons and Cup | 1 teaspoon (ts) | 1 tablespoon (Ts) | 1 cup |
|---|---|---|---|
| Water Liquor Milk | 5 g | 15 g | 200 g |
| Refined Sugar | 3 | 9 | 120 |
| Granulated Sugar | 4 | 12 | 170 |
| Confectioners' Sugar | 3 | 8 | 100 |
| Soft Wheat Flour | 2.5 | 8 | 100 |
| Butter Oil | 4 | 13 | 180 |
| Salt | 5 | 15 | 200 |
| Ground Almonds | 2.5 | 7 | 85 |
| Baking Powder | 3.5 | 10 | – |
| Baking Soda | 3.5 | 10 | – |
| Cocoa | 2 | 6 | 80 |
| Cinnamon | 5 | 15 | – |
| Heavy Cream | 5 | 15 | 200 |
| Egg (One unshelled egg is about 50 g.) | Egg Yolk 18~20 g | Egg White 30~32 g | |

This is based on level measurement of filling a measuring cup or a spoon.

## HELPFUL HINTS FOR MAKING COOKIES

Make small amount of cookies at a time. Cookies are most flavorful when removed from the oven. They will lose crispiness and flavor as they become old.

**HOW TO CREAM BUTTER:** If butter is not beaten well, baked cookies will not be crispy. Have butter at room temperature (about 24°C) before you use. Beat butter until light and fluffy trapping air as much as possible.

**HOW TO ADD SUGAR:** When adding sugar to butter, add one half or one third at a time.

**HOW TO ADD EGGS:** If you add eggs all at one, it is hard to mix with butter. A large amount of eggs cool butter and make it hard. Add a small amount of eggs at a time and mix well.

**REST DOUGH:** After making dough, refrigerate for about 20 minutes to rest. While resting, flour and butter are mixed well. In addition, chilled dough is easy to roll out and cut out.

**DON'T FLOUR TOO MUCH:** For dusting a board or hands use as little flour as possible. Too much flour makes crust stiff and ruins taste.

**PREHEAT OVEN 20 MINUTES BEFORE USING:** As this is explained before, preheat the oven to obtain the indicated temperature.

## PREPARE ALL NECESSARY INGREDIENTS AND UTENSILS BEFORE YOU START.

Wear an apron and hair scarf. Wash your hands. Clean up your kitchen and the working table. Measure all the required ingredients accurately. If you measure the ingredients while cooking, sometimes it is too late to add, which will cause a failure. Dirty utensils also will fail to make dough properly. Wash and dry the necessary utensils before you start. Clean them again after finishing for the next use.

# Various Sablés...*Crumbly and tasty cookies.*

*Home-made cookies are popular now. Enjoy baking cookies.*

## Ingredients (Makes 15 sablés)

For Dough A:
- 100 g   soft wheat flour;
- 80 g   butter;
- Pinch of salt;
- 40 g   confectioners' sugar;
- Grated lemon rind;
- $\frac{1}{2}$   egg.

Hard wheat flour for dustings.

For B: Same as Dough A; 1 Ts instant coffee and hot water to dissolve coffee.

For C: Same as Dough A but reduce flour to 90 g and add 10 g cocoa.

For D: Same as Dough A; Apricot jam to glaze.

For E: Same as Dough A; 1 ts sesame seeds; Granulated sugar to sprinkle.

Cream butter and salt with wire whisk and add confectioners' sugar and mix well.

Stir in grated lemon rind and lightly beaten egg.

Fold in sifted flour with wooden spatula. Place dough in plastic bag and refrigerate for 20 minutes to rest.

Roll out dough into 4 mm thickness on floured pastry cloth.

Cut out rolled dough into desired shapes with cookie cutters and make dots or designs with bamboo stick. Bake in 160–170°C preheated oven for about 12–13 minutes or until lightly browned.

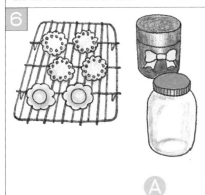

Cool on wire racks and store in airtight containers.

### Variation B:

Add dissolved coffee to butter mixture at step 2 and make as for A.

### Variation C:

Fold in sifted flour with cocoa at step 3 and make as for A.

### Variation D:

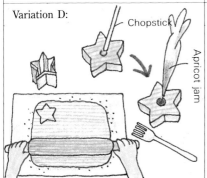

At step 4, score parallel lines over rolled dough with checker roller or fork. Cut out, hollow at center and fill in apricot jam.

### Variation E:

Add sesame seeds to dough at step 3. Sprinkle granulated sugar after cutting out and bake.

## Cookie, Biscuit, and Sablé— Do you know the difference?

Cookie is a small cake made from sweet stiff dough. Biscuit is a small cake of quick bread raised with baking powder or soda. Sablé is a cookie originally made in Normandy and means "sandy" in French.

# Almond Sablés...*Flavorful cookies.*

*Make your original designs and send them to your friends.*

## Ingredients (Makes 25 sablés)

For Dough A:
- 150g    soft wheat flour;
- 100g    butter;
- 60g     sugar;
- 20g     egg;
- 40g     ground almonds;
- ½ ts    baking powder

Hard wheat flour for dusting.

For Finishing:
- For Glaze: 1 egg yolk and 1 ts water.
- Poppy seeds for C.

**1 | A**

Cream butter until light and fluffy, then add sugar, one half at a time and mix well.

**2**

Stir in lightly beaten egg.

**3**

Add ground almonds and fold in sifted flour and baking powder.

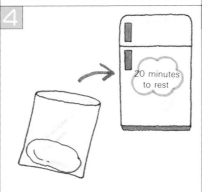

**4**

Place in plastic bag and refrigerate for 20 minutes to rest.

**5**

Roll out dough into 4 mm thickness on floured pastry cloth.

**6**

Cut out into desired shapes with cookie cutters. Brush diluted egg yolk over surface and score lines or draw designs with fork or bamboo stick.

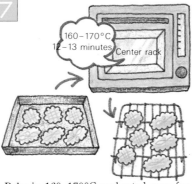

**7**

160–170°C
12–13 minutes
Center rack

Bake in 160–170°C preheated oven for 12–13 minutes. Cool on wire racks and store in airtight containers.

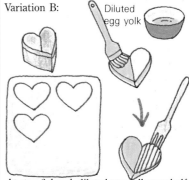

**Variation B:**

At step 6, brush diluted egg yolk over half of surface and score lines on the other half.

**Variation C:**

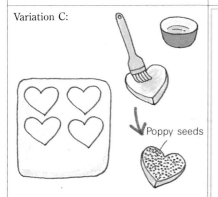

After brushing egg yolk over surface, sprinkle poppy seeds and bake.

**Q & A**

**Why does dough need resting?** When various ingredients are mixed, some of them change their original natures. If you rest dough for some time, you can handle, roll out and cut out dough quite easily. This is because all ingredients are blended well while resting. If you use dough without resting, you can not roll out dough smoothly. Place dough in plastic bag and seal to prevent forming crust. Much butter is used for making cookies, so it is important to chill butter in the dough for easy handling.

# Frosted Sablés...Color icing and decorate sablés.

*After you are accustomed to baking, frost cookies with lovely designs.*

**Ingredients (Makes 20 sablés)**

For Dough:
- 125 g   soft wheat flour;
- 90 g   butter;
- Pinch of salt;
- 40 g   sugar;
- 1   egg yolk
- Few drops of vanilla oil.

For Royal Icing:
- 100 g   confectioners' sugar;
- 25 c.c.   egg white;
- Few drops of lemon juice.
- Food colors (Use favorite colors.)

**1**

Cream butter and salt until light and fluffy, then add sugar one half at a time and mix well.

**2**

Stir in egg yolk and vanilla oil.

**3**

Fold in sifted flour. Place dough in plastic bag and refrigerate for 20 minutes to rest.

**4**

Roll out dough into 4 mm thickness on floured pastry cloth.

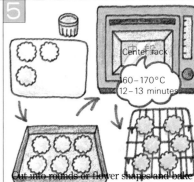

**5**

Cut into rounds or flower shapes and bake in 160–170°C preheated oven for 12–13 minutes. Remove onto wire racks and cool.

**For Royal Icing:**

**1**

Add egg white to confectioners' sugar and mix well with spoon.

**2**

Blend in a few drops of lemon juice. Divide icing into three or four cups.

**3**

Color each cup with desired color.

**4**

Spread icing over baked cookies and pipe lines or dots.

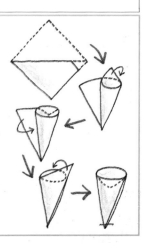

## How to decorate cookies with icing:

Use disposable pastry bags for decorating cookies with icing as well as brushes. Hold a pastry bag in an upright position, 2 cm above a cookie, and pipe designs. Practice piping lines, small flowers or letters on wax paper before piping on cookies. Fold a sheet of paraffin paper as shown and make a disposable bag. Make bags as many as the required number of colors. When completely dry, icing becomes shiny.

11

# Macaroons...

*Form into balls with your hands. Easy to make for the clumsy.*

B

A

## Party Beverages (Individual serving)

*Yogurt Drink:*

150 g unsweetened yo-gurt; 1 Ts raspberry jam; 1 ts lemon juice; 70 c.c. water. Mix all in-gredients well and pour into glass with ice cubes.

*Orange Juice:*

150 c.c. orange juice; 1 Ts honey juice. Mix all ingredients and pour into glass with ice cubes. Garnish with a cherry and a segment of orange.

*Peppermint Milk:*

Mix 200 c.c. milk and 15 c.c. peppermint well. Pour into glass with ice cubes. Garnish with cherries and serve with syrup.

## Ingredients (Makes 25 macaroons)

For Dough A:
- 100 g crunchy peanut butter;
- 50 g walnuts;
- 100 g granulated sugar;
- Ground cinnamon;
- 30 c.c. egg white.
- Egg white for forming.

For B:
- 100 g shredded coconuts;
- 80 g granulated sugar;
- 1 ts cocoa.
- Egg white for forming.
- Shredded coconuts for coating.

**1 A**

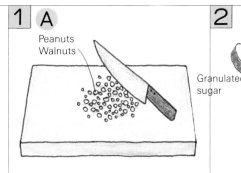

Chop peanuts and walnuts to be as small as possible.

**2**

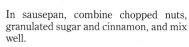

In sausepan, combine chopped nuts, granulated sugar and cinnamon, and mix well.

**3**

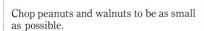

Add egg white and mix.

**4**

Over low heat, cook to make thick paste, constantly stirring.

**5**

Remove from heat and cool to 36–37°C. Shape into small balls, one at a time, applying egg white onto your hands.

**6**

Place balls onto foil-lined cookie sheets and rest for 20 minutes. Bake in 150°C preheated oven for about 20 minutes.

**Variation B:**

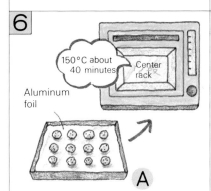

Chop shredded coconuts into small pieces. Reserve some for coating.

**1 2**

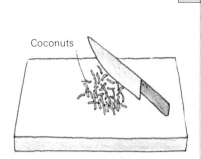

Mix coconuts, granulated sugar and cocoa in saucepan. Cook and make following steps 3 to 5.

**3**

Cover each ball with shredded coconuts and bake following step 6.

## How to join white and brown doughs to make checkers. The following care must be taken to ensure a smooth surface:

① When you make a square bar with dough, make the required shape with cardboard first and fit dough into cardboard shape. Then wrap and refrigerate to chill.
② Brush milk over surface of joining and put brown and white rectangles together.

Cover with cardboard to make sharp corners and refrigerate again.
③ If dough is refrigerated too long, it is hard to smooth out. Leave dough at room temperature for some time, then cut with a knife.

# Plain Icebox Cookies...

*When you have time, make dough and freeze. Bake anytime you like.*

## Beverages (Individual serving)

### Iced Tea:

Place 1 ts tea leaves in a preheated pot, pour 150c.c. boiling water and allow the leaves to steep for 3 minutes. Pour tea over cubed ice. Serve with a slice lemon and syrup.

### Iced Coffee:

Pour 150c.c. hot coffee over cubed ice. Serve with syrup and light cream.

*How to make syrup:*

Put same amount of sugar and water in saucepan and dissolve sugar over low heat. Remove from heat and cool.

Sugar

Wate

14

Ingredients (Makes 15 cookies)
For Dough A:
    110g  soft wheat flour;
    80g   butter;
    40g   sugar;
    1      egg yolk.
Hard flour for dustings.
For B: 1 Ts instant coffee and hot water to dissolve; Slivered almonds for coating.
For C: Same as A, but reduce 10g flour and add 10g cocoa; Granulated sugar.
For D: Royal icing (150g confectioners' sugar; 12 c.c. egg white; Few drops of lemon juice). See page 11 for making. Orange peel for topping.

**1 A**

Cream butter until light and fluffy, then add sugar half at a time and mix well.

**2**

Stir in egg yolk.

**3**

Fold in sifted flour with wooden spatula.

**4**

Place dough in plastic bag and refrigerate for 20 minutes to rest.

**5**

Roll dough into cylinder shape, 3cm in diameter. Wrap with brown paper and refrigerate for 2 hours.

**6**

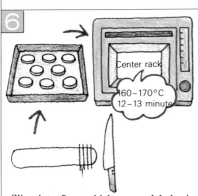

Slice into 5mm thickness and bake in 160-170°C preheated oven for 12-13 minutes.

Variation B:

Stir in dissolved instant coffee at step 2.

**1 2**

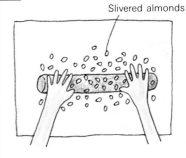

Roll dough over chopped almonds at step 6. Slice and bake in same way.

Variation C:

**1 2**

Fold in sifted flour and cocoa at step 3. Follow steps 4 and 5.

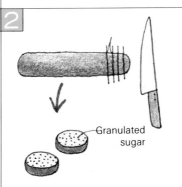

After slicing into 5mm thickness, sprinkle granulated sugar over top of each round. Bake in same way.

Variation D:

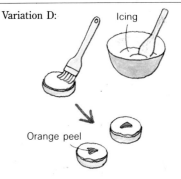

After baked cookies become cool, brush icing over top of each round and decorate with orange peel.

# Checkers...

Boy's and Girl's Faces. Make white and brown doughs. Join them as shown.

16

## Ingredients (Makes 15 cookies)

For White Dough:
- 100g  soft wheat flour;
- 80g  butter;
- 50g  sugar;
- 1  egg yolk (large).

For Brown Dough:
- Use 90g soft wheat flour and add 10g cocoa. Other ingredients are same as white dough.

Hard wheat flour for dusting.

Milk for joining.

For F and G:  Candied cherries for mouth.

**1**

Make white and brown doughs individually following steps 1–4 and C1 on page 15. Shape into square bars and refrigerate for 20 minutes to rest.

**2**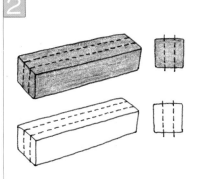

Divide each dough into three lengthwise.

**3**

Brush milk over surface to be joined. Join brown and white doughs as shown and refrigerate for 2 hours.

**4**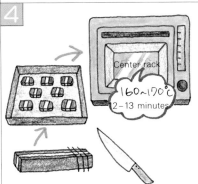

Slice into 5mm thickness and bake in 160–170°C preheated oven for 12–13 minutes.

### Variation B:

Roll out brown dough into 2mm thickness and cover white-brown-white dough with rolled dough. Refrigerate again to rest. Slice and bake as for A.

### Variations C and D:
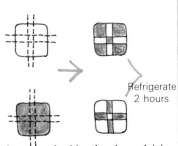

Cut brown and white doughs and join them as shown, brushing milk for joining. Refrigerate for 2 hours, slice and bake.

### Variation E:

Join as shown and wrap with rolled brown dough. Refrigerate for 2 hours, slice and bake.

### Variation F:
**1**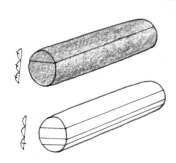

Cut brown and white cylinder doughs as shown.

**2**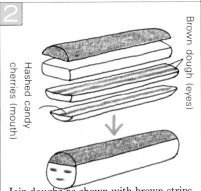

Join doughs as shown with brown strips for eyes and cherry strip for mouth in place, brushing milk for joining.

### Variation G:

Join doughs as for F. Refrigerate to rest.

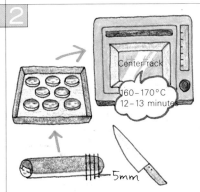

Slice into 5mm thickness. Bake at 160–170°C for 12–13 minutes.

17

# Spiced Cookies for Tree Ornaments...

When Christmas is near at hand, Scandinavian people bake spiced cookies and hang them on the walls, doors and Christmas tree. The house is filled with good smell of cookies. If cookie cutters are not available, make patterns with cardboard. These cookies will keep for two months.

## Ingredients (Makes 15 cookies)

For Dough:
- 100g   soft wheat flour;
- 30g   butter;
- 40g   sugar;
- 1g   baking soda;   25c.c.  water
- $\frac{1}{2}$ ts   ground cinnamon;
- $\frac{1}{4}$ ts   ground cloves;
- $\frac{1}{4}$ ts   ground ginger;
- $\frac{1}{4}$ ts   cocoa.

Hard wheat flour for dusting.

For Decorating:
Royal icing (see page 11 for making):
- 100g   confectioners' sugar;
- 25c.c.  egg white;   Few drops of lemon juice.

Food colors. Silver dragees.

**1**

Cream butter until light and fluffy, then add sugar and mix well.

**2**

Stir in dissolved soda with water.

**3**

Fold in sifted flour, spices and cocoa with wooden spatula.

**4**

Place dough in plastic bag and refrigerate for 20 minutes to trst.

**5**

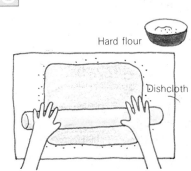

Roll out into 3mm thickness on floured surface. Cut out into desired shapes.

**6**

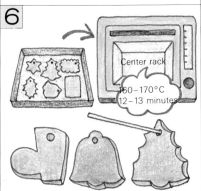

Make hole at top of each cookie for hanging.

**7**

Make icing. Pipe designs on baked cookies.

## Actual-size Patterns

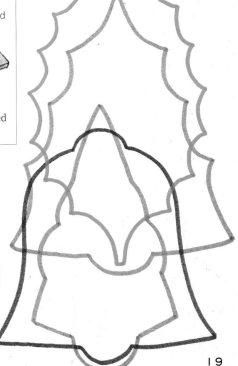

# Cookie House...

This house is disassembled at Christmas' night after exchanging Christmas greetings. Making a cookie is a regular event of my family. Let's bake cookies to make a fancy house.

## Ingredients

Make dough following instructions on page 19.

- 200g  soft wheat flour;
- 60g  butter;
- 80g  sugar;
- 2g  baking soda;  50c.c. water
- 1 ts  ground cinnamon;
- $\frac{1}{2}$ ts  ground cloves;
- $\frac{1}{2}$ ts  ground ginger;
- $\frac{1}{2}$ ts  cocoa.

Hard wheat flour for dusting.

### For Decoration:

Royal icing (see page 11 for making):
- 150g  confectioners' sugar;
- 40c.c. egg white;  Few drops of lemon juice.

Confectioners' sugar.   Sprigs of fir.

**1**

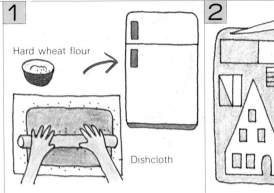

Hard wheat flour

Dishcloth

Roll out dough into 3mm thickness. Refrigerate to rest.

**2**

Cut out pieces with knife using cardboard patterns.

**3**

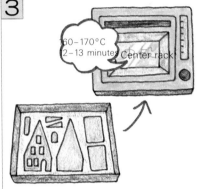

160-170°C
12-13 minutes  Center rack

Bake in 160-170°C preheated oven for 12-13 minutes.

**4**

Roof

Icing

Pipe dots and zigzag lines on front piece as shown. Attach window sills with icing. Brush icing all over roof and pipe designs as shwon.

**5**

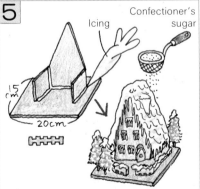

Icing

Confectioner's sugar

15 cm

20cm

Assemble house with icing for joining. Sprinkle confectioners' sugar over house.

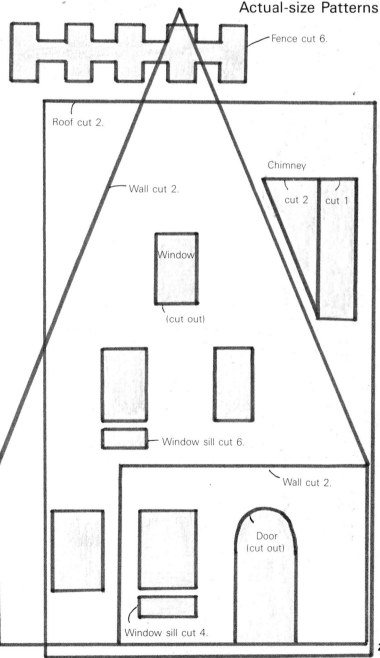

## Actual-size Patterns

Fence cut 6.

Roof cut 2.

Wall cut 2.

Chimney

cut 2   cut 1

Window

(cut out)

Window sill cut 6.

Wall cut 2.

Door
(cut out)

Window sill cut 4.

# Shortcake...

*Make gorgeous shortcake with easy-to-make cookies.*

Tag for message is made from remaining dough. Pack assorted cookies you bake following recipes in this book and send for a gift.

## Ingredients

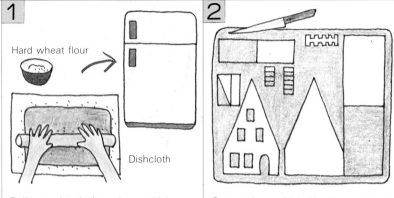

Ingredients (Makes three 15 cm-diameter cookies)

For Dough:
- 225 g  soft wheat flour;
- 130 g  butter;
- 90 g  sugar;
- 30 g  egg;
- 60 g  ground almonds;
- $2/3$ ts  baking powder.

Hard wheat flour for dusting.

For decoration:
Whipped cream:
- 150 g  heavy cream;
- 15 g  sugar;
- Kirsch.

Strawberries. Chocolate for letters.

**1**

Sugar

Butter

Cream butter until light and fluffy, then add sugar one third at a time and mix well.

**2**

Egg

Stir in lightly beaten egg.

**3**

Soft wheat flour with baking powder.

Ground almonds

Fold in sifted flour, ground almonds and baking powder.

**4**

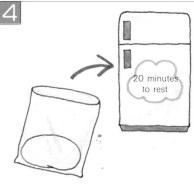

20 minutes to rest

Place dough in plastic bag and refrigerate for 20 minutes to rest.

**5**

Flour for dusting.

Divide dough into three and roll out into 4–5 mm thickness on floured surface.

**6**

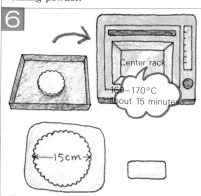

Center rack

160–170°C about 15 minutes

←15cm→

Cut out into 15 cm diameter rounds with scalloped cookie cutter. Bake in 160–170°C preheated oven for 15 minutes.

**7**

Whipped cream

Heavy cream
Sugar

Kirsch

Ice water

To make whipped cream, beat heavy cream, sugar over ice water and kirsch until peaks form.

**8**

Spread whipped cream over top of cookie and arrange strawberries. Repeat for the second layer.

**9**

Write letters with chocolate.

HAPPY BIRTHDAY

Pipe whipped cream on top and arrange strawberries as shown. Place rectangle cookie tag with chocolate letters at center.

Note:

When cookie cutters are not available, a doll house and some shapes from a picture book are needed. You can make patterns as shown below. Bake your picture into cookies and send to your friends.

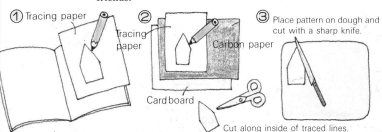

① Tracing paper

② Tracing paper — Carbon paper

③ Place pattern on dough and cut with a sharp knife

Cardboard

Cut along inside of traced lines

*Kirsch: For Muslims, use only essence and don't use any liquor.

## Ingredients (Makes 15 cookies)

For Dough:
   125 g   soft wheat flour;
   80 g   butter;
   Pinch of salt;
   40 g   sugar;
   1   egg yolk;
   Vanilla oil.
Hard wheat flour for dusting

For Finishing:
   Apricot jam;
   Raspberry jam;
   Confectioners' sugar.
Make dough following steps 1–3 on page 11.

**1**

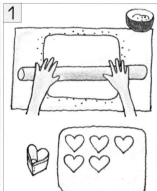

Roll out dough into 2–3 mm thickness on floured surface. Cut out with heart-shaped cutter.

**2**

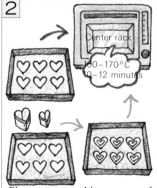

Place cut out cookies on greased cookie sheets. Cut out small hearts from bigger ones. Bake in 160–170°C preheated oven for 10–12 minutes.

**3**

Brush jam over lower pieces while cookies are warm. Sprinkle confectioners' sugar over upper pieces. Put lower and upper pieces together after upper pieces are cool.

24

Ingredients (Makes 15 cookies)

For Dough:
  Same as dough on opposite page.
For Decoration:
  Chocolate;
  Royal icing (see page 11 for making)
  Food colors.
Make dough following steps 1–3 on page 11.

Practice piping letters before you pipe on cookies. Make heart-shaped cardboard pattern if the cutter is not available.

**1** Flour for dusting

Roll out dough into 4–5 mm thickness on floured surface. Cut out with heart-shaped cutter.

**2** 160–170°C
12–13 minutes Center rack

Chocolate

Bake in 160–170°C preheated oven for 12–13 minutes. Melt chocolate over hot water.

**3** Icing

Pour melted chocolate over cookies. After they are completely dry, pipe letters or designs with icing as you like.

25

# Peter Rabbit Cottontail...Rabbit family enjoys picnic lunch.

*Make patterns from your favorite pictures and bake cookies with children.*

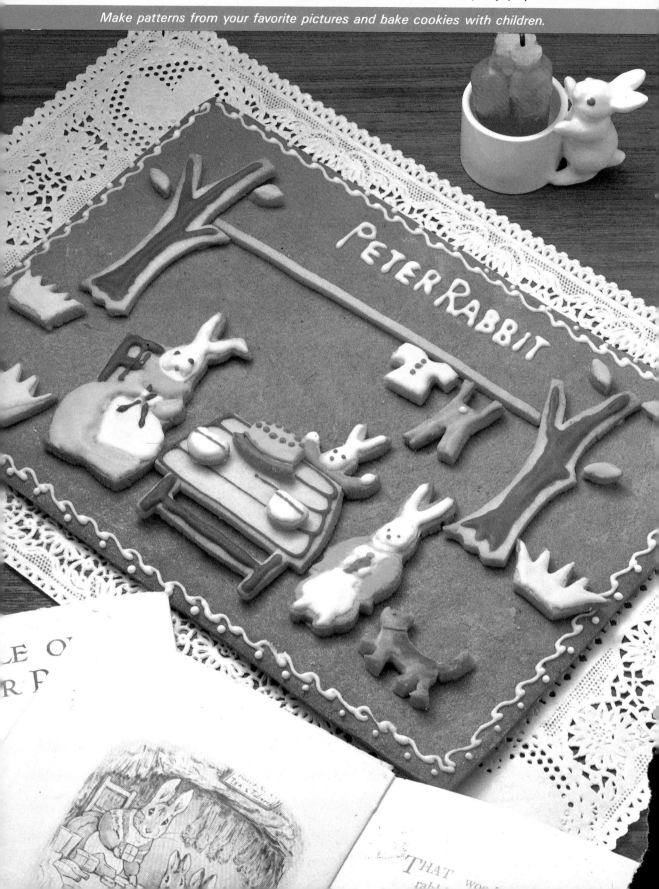

## Ingredients

For White Dough:
Make dough following steps 1–4 on page 15.

- 300 g   soft wheat flour;
- 150 g   butter;
- 20 g   sugar;
- 60 g   egg.

For Brown Dough:
Same as white dough, but add 5 g cocoa.
Hard wheat flour for dusting.

For Decoration:

For Royal icing:
- 120 g   confectioners' sugar;
- 30 c.c.   egg white;   Few drops of lemon juice.

Food colors.

**1** Transfer actual-size patterns onto cardboard following directions on page 23 and cut out.

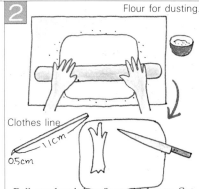

**2** Flour for dusting.

Clothes line

11 cm

0.5 cm

Roll out dough into 3 mm thickness. Cut out shapes with sharp knife using cardboard patterns. Cut out clothes line, too.

**3** Cookie board

Center rack

160–170°C
12–13 minutes

20 cm
15 cm

Bake in 160–170°C preheated oven for 12–13 minutes.

**4** Icing

Color royal icing and pipe designs as shown.

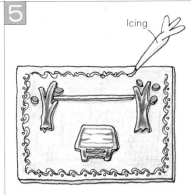

**5** Icing

Attach shapes with icing onto cookie board.

Actual-size
Patterns

Leaf
Cut 5.

Cup
Cut 2.

Cake

Grass Cut 3.

# Doll House... *How about making a doll house?*

## Ingredients

For Dough: See steps 1–4 on page 15.
- 300 g  soft wheat flour;
- 150 g  butter;
- 120 g  sugar;
- 60 g  egg.

Hard wheat flour for dusting.

## For Finishing:

Royal icing (see page 11 for making)
- 150 g  confectioners' sugar;
- 40 c.c. egg white;
- Few drops of lemon juice.

Food colors.
Silver dragees.
Chocolate.

Make cardboard pattern as simple as possible. It is hard to bake complicated shapes with slits or cut-outs.

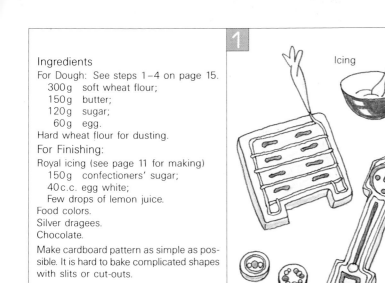

**1** Icing

Bake required shapes as for Rabbit's picture on page 27. Decorate with icing as shown on the opposite page.

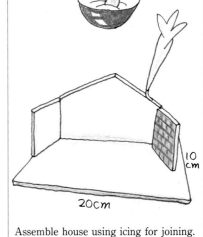

**2**

10 cm

20 cm

Assemble house using icing for joining.

## Actual-size Patterns

Roof cut 2.

Plate for top shelf

Mirror

Chest

Side of mantelpiece cut 2.

Top of mantelpiece.

Ornament

Plate for cupboard cut 6.

Wall cut 2.

Grandfather's clock

Door (cut out)

Window (cut out)

Top of cupboard and shelf cut each 3.

Top of chest } cut
Shelf above window } each 1

Side of cupboard cut 2.

Door for cupboard

Plate    Plate

Baby's face

Cake

Plate

Kettle

Leg of table cut 4.

Chair cut 4.

Dog

Dog's dish

Cradle cut 2.

29

# Tartlets...Decorate with various fruits in season.

## These decorated tartlets make any party delightful.

## Ingredients (Makes 15 tartlets)

For Dough:  See steps 1–4 on page 15.
- 180g   soft wheat flour;
- 120g   butter;
- 80g   confectioners' sugar;
- 1   egg yolk;
- Vanilla oil.

For Custard Cream:
- 2   egg yolk;
- 30g   sugar;
- 1 Ts   soft wheat flour;
- 1 Ts   cornstarch;
- 200 c.c. milk
- Vanilla extract;
- 1 Ts   liqueur.

For Whipped Cream:
- 150g   heavy cream;
- 15g   sugar;
- Kirsch.

For Topping:
- For A: Apricot jam; Raspberry jam; Strawberries; Custard cream.
- For B: Cherries (canned); Whipped cream.
- For C: Blackberries (canned); Whipped cream.
- For D: Kiwi fruit.
- For E: Peaches (canned).
- For F: Pineapples (canned); Custard cream and whipped cream for D, E and F.

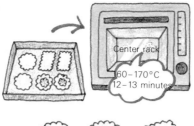

Roll out dough into 3mm thickness. Cut out into rounds and rectangles. Bake in 160–170°C preheated oven for 12–13 minutes.

**1**

Custard cream

In saucepan, combine egg yolk, 1 Ts milk, sugar, flour and cornstarch.

**2**

Warm milk 60°C

Warm milk to 60°C and add to egg mixture. Cook over low heat, stirring constantly.

**3**

Liqueur

Vanilla

Remove from heat. After it is cool, add liqueur and vanilla.

**A**
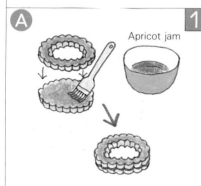

Apricot jam

Brush apricot jam over surface of each cookie and put two cookies together.

**1  2**

Custard cream

Dip strawberries in raspberry jam.

Pipe custard cream into center hole. Dip strawberries in raspberry jam and place on top.

Variations B & C:
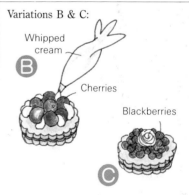

Whipped cream

**B**

Cherries

Blackberries

**C**

Place cherries or blackberries on top and pipe whipped cream.

Variations D, E & F:

**D**    Kiwi    **F**

Custard cream

Pineapples

Peachs    **E**

Brush jam over rectangles, spread custard cream, place fruits and pipe whipped cream.

Q&A

### How to store cookies:

Cool baked cookies on wire racks. Then store them in airtight containers. If available, put desiccant in it. Don't keep baked cookies for a long time. Eat them up in a week or so. They will lose flavor of butter and crispiness as they become old. Make as much as you need at a time. You can freeze dough of icebox cookies.

*Liqueur, kirsh: For Muslims, use only essence and don't use any liquor.

# Butter Cookies...Good treat for tea time.

*It does not take time to bake these cookies.*

**Ingredients (Makes 30 cookies)**

For Batter:
- 200g   soft wheat flour;
- 120g   butter;
- 80g   confectioners' sugar;
- Grated lemon rind;
- 1   egg.

For Topping
- For A: Candied cherries
- For B: Angelica
- For C: Raisins
- For D: Use 180g soft wheat flour and 20g cocoa.

**1**

Cream butter until light and fluffy, then add sugar one third at a time and mix well.

**2**

Grated lemon rind

Stir in grated lemon rind and egg.

**3**

Soft wheat flour

Fold in sifted flour with wooden spatula.

**4**

(A)

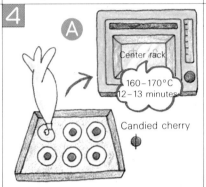

Center rack
160–170°C
12–13 minutes

Candied cherry

Shape into rings onto cookie sheets with pastry bag. Place halved cherry at center of each ring.

**Variation B:**

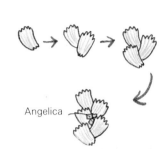

Angelica

Form shapes as shown piping on the right and left alternately. Place chopped angelica at center and bake.

**Variation C:**

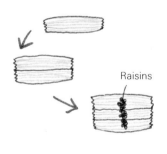

Raisins

Pipe 3 logs side by side. Place chopped raisins at center and bake.

**Variation D:**

Soft wheat flour
Cocoa

Fold in sifted flour and cocoa at step 3.

**12**

Form into ring with pastry bag. Make a star on joint.

---

Q & A

## How to make well-formed cookies with pastry bag:

It is easy to make cookies using a pastry bag, for you don't have to wait to rest dough. Fill pastry bag with batter and press bag onto cookie sheets forming desired shapes. If batter is too soft, it will flow and cannot retain trace of metal tube. If batter is too hard, you cannot press. Measure all ingredients accurately and keep in mind to the followings.

① Preheat oven until required temperature is obtained. Bake as soon as you make shapes onto cookie sheets.

② Beat butter until light and fluffy, trapping air as much as possible.

③ Add confectioners' sugar one third at a time. Beat well until there is no lump.

④ Sift flour before you mix with other ingredients. Fold in sifted flour with a wooden spatula.

⑤ Don't stop pressing until one shape is formed.

⑥ Bake at once. If you leave shaped batter for a long time, batter will be soft and lose original design.

# Raisin Sablés... *Sandwiches. Taste rum flavor of these rich cookies.*

*Crumbly sablés make sophisticated snadwiches. Serve with tea.*

## Ingredients (Makes 10 sablé sandwiches)

For Dough (see page 9 for making):
- 150g soft wheat flour;
- 100g butter;
- 60g sugar;
- 20g egg;
- 40g ground almonds;
- 1/2 ts baking powder.

Hard wheat four for dusting.

For Filling Buttercream:
- 100g unsalted butter;
- 30g sugar; 15c.c. water;
- 1 Ts rum;
- Vanilla extract.

For Glaze: Raisins soaked in rum. 1 egg yolk and water. Slivered almonds for topping.

**1**

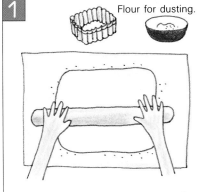

Roll out dough into 3-4 mm thickness. Cut out into rectangles.

**2**

Brush diluted egg yolk on surface and place slivered almonds on top of upper pieces.

**3**

To make buttercream, cream butter until light and fluffy.

**4**

In saucepan, dissolve sugar in water and heat to make syrup. Leave to cool.

**5**

Add syrup gradually into creamed butter and stir.

**6**

Add vanilla and rum.

**7**

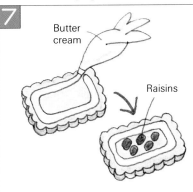

Pipe buttercream onto lower pieces and place raisins at center.

**8**

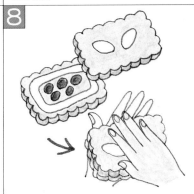

Place upper pieces on lower ones and press lightly.

---

### How to brew tea:

Nothing is so flavorful as freshly brewed tea. Brew tea following directions below.

Note:

①

Place tea leaves, 1 ts tea leaves per a cup plus 1 ts in preheated pot.

②

Pour boiling water, 150c.c. per a cup, into the pot.

③ About 3 minutes.

Allow leaves to steep for about 3 minutes.

④

Pour tea through a preheated sieve into each cup.

※Rum: For Muslims, use only essence and don't use any liquor.

# Florentines...Send rich cookies to your friends.

*Topped with honeyed nuts and dried fruits, they are gorgeous cookies.*

**Ingredients (Makes 20 florentines)**
For Dough: (See page 14 for making)
   255 g  soft wheat flour;
   120 g  butter;
   100 g  confectioners' sugar;
    40 g  egg.
Hard wheat flour for dusting.

For Topping:
    75 g  sugar;
  150 c.c. rum;
    75 g  honey;
    30 g  butter;
    50 g  slivered almonds;
Candied cherries;
Raisins.

**1**

Make dough following directions on page 14 and roll out into 4–5 mm thickness on floured surface.

**2**
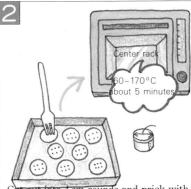
Cut out into 4 cm rounds and prick with fork. Bake in 160–170°C preheaed oven for about 5 minutes.

**3**

In saucepan combine sugar, rum and honey. Place pan over low heat.

**4**

Cook to thicken, brushing side of pan with water occasionally.

**5**

Cook until mixture pull thread between chopsticks, 3 cm a part.

**6**

Add butter, slivered almonds and dried fruits and mix them well.

**7**

Place honeyed almonds and fruits on top of each cookie.

**8**
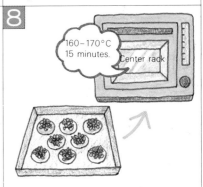
Bake at 160–170°C preheated oven for about 15 minutes.

## Helpful Hints for Gift Packaging:

Tie with ribbon bow.

When you have mastered making cookies, you may feel like sending home-made cookies to your friends. Here are some ideas for packaging cookies. Tie ribbon around bottle neck and make bow. Attach letter stickers or label onto jar. Make embroidered lid cover and wrap lid.

Keep empty fancy cans and boxes for gift packaging.

Pack cookies with candies and jellies.

Place lacy paper on rattan plate, place cookies and wrap with cellophane.

Place each cookie in individual foil case or paper cup.

Decorate box with fancy paper and attach lacy paper along edges.

Make innr bag with paraffin paper and insert into paper bag.

※Rum: For Muslims, use only essence and don't use any liquor.

# Pies... *These are salty pies, topped with cheese, seaweed or paprika.*

*Good for snack and hor d'oeuvre with drinks. Don't stir dough!*

## Ingredients (Makes 15 pies)

For Dough:
  150g  soft wheat flour;
  Pinch of salt;
  120g  butter;
  50c.c. ice water.
Hard wheat flour for dusting.

For Topping:
  1 egg yolk and 1 ts water for glaze.
For A: Grated cheese
For B: Dried seaweed
For C: Paprika

### 1

Soft wheat flour
Salt
Butter
Pastry cutter

In bowl, sift flour and salt together. Cut butter into flour mixture with pastry cutter.

### 2

Pea size
Ice water

Cut butter until it is pea size. Add ice water one third or a quarter at a time and mix dough with fingertips.

### 3
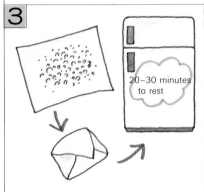
20–30 minutes to rest

Wrap dough with dry towel and refrigerate for 20–30 minutes to rest.

### 4
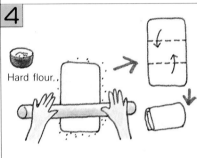
Hard flour

Roll out dough into rectangle on floured surface. Fold one third each from both sides.

### 5
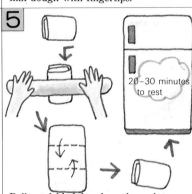
20–30 minutes to rest

Roll out folded dough as shown into rectangle and fold again. Refrigerate for 20–30 minutes to rest.

### 6
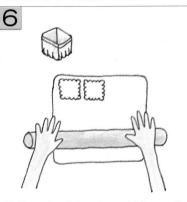

Roll out dough into 5mm thickness. Cut into squares with cutter.

### 7

Diluted egg yolk
Cheese
 A

Brush diluted egg yolk onto surface and spread grated cheese.

### 8
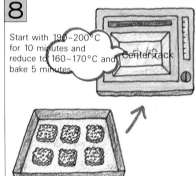
Start with 190–200°C for 10 minutes and reduce to 160–170°C and bake 5 minutes.
Center rack

Bake in 190–200°C preheated oven for 10 minutes, reduce heat to 160–170°C and bake for 5 minutes.

## Variations:
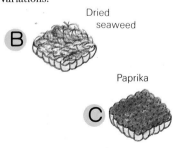
Dried seaweed
B

Paprika
C

Place dried seaweed for B and sprinkle paprika for C. Bake in same way.

## Q&A

### How to bake a flaky pie:

Tasty pies have layers of flaky crust. By repeating folding and rolling, layers are made in dough. Handle pie dough as quickly as possible taking care of the followings.

① Cut chilled butter into flour with pastry cutter. Work as quickly as possible to prevent butter from melting.
② Don't knead dough when water is added. Mix dough as lightly as possible and refrigerate to chill. Always keep pie dough cool.

# Icebox Cookies...

*You can bake tasty cookies using toaster oven.*

## Ingredients (Makes 15 cookies)

For Dough A:
- 110g    soft wheat flour;
- 70g    butter;
- 50g    sugar;
- 1½    eggs;
- 5g    each of chopped angelica, raisins and candied cherries.

Hard wheat flour for dusting.
Chopped almonds and egg white for coating.

For Dough B:
- 100g    soft wheat flour;
- 50g    butter;
- 40g    sugar;
- 20g    egg;
- Grated lemon rind (use ½ lemon).

Hard wheat flour for dusting.

For Decoration:
Royal Icing:
- 50g    confectioners' sugar;
- 12c.c.    egg white;
- Few drops of lemon juice.

Apricot jam and silver dragees.

When you bake cookies using toaster oven for the first time, check temperature and baking time occasionally. You cannot bake lots of cookies at a time. Keep remaining dough in freezer.

**1 A**

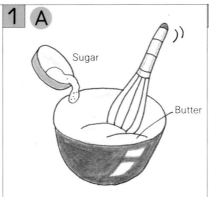

Cream butter until light and fluffy, then add sugar one half at a time and mix well.

**2**

Stir in lightly beaten eggs, one third or a quarter at a time.

**3**

Add chopped dried fruits and fold in sifted flour.

**4**

Place dough in plastic bag and refrigerate for 20 minutes to rest.

**5**

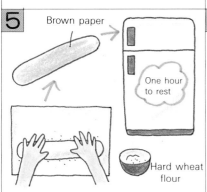

Roll dough into cylindrical shape and wrap with brown paper. Refrigerate for one hour.

**6**

Brush egg white all around dough and sprinkle chopped almonds all over.

**7 A**

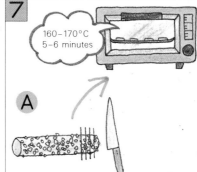

Slice into 5mm thickness and bake in 160-170°C preheated toaster oven for 5-6 minutes.

**Variation B:**

**1**

At step 3, substitute grated lemon rind for dried fruits. Roll out into rectangle and cut out shapes with cutters.

**2**

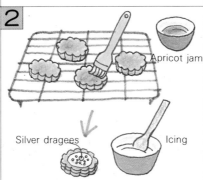

Brush apricot jam over surface. Spread icing and sprinkle silver dragees on top.

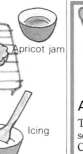

Note

## About Toaster Oven:

Toaster oven cannot produce high power, so bake small amount of cookies at a time. Carefully read manufacturers pamphlet and adjust heat to obtain indicated temperature.

41

# Ⓐ Ladyfingers and Ⓑ Charlottes...

*These are soft and spongy cookies.*

Ⓐ

Ⓑ

## Ingredients (Makes 25 ladyfingers)

For Dough:
- 50 g soft wheat flour;
- 15 g cornstarch;
- 2 egg yolks;
- 30 g sugar;
- 2 egg whites;
- 20 g sugar;
- small amount of grated lemon rind;
- 1/2 ts baking powder.
- Confectioners' sugar.

For Charlottes:

For Bavarian cream: (16 cm in diameter)
- 10 g gelatin; (made from whale)
- 60 c.c. water;
- 400 c.c. milk;
- 160 g sugar;
- 4 egg yolks;
- Vanilla extract;
- 2 Ts liqueur;
- 200 c.c. heavy cream.

For Decoration:
- Whipped cream (150 g heavy cream;
- 15 g sugar; Few drops of kirsch)
- Ribbon

**For Ladyfingers:**

Combine egg yolks and sugar and beat well.

Beat egg whites until peaks form. Add sugar and beat.

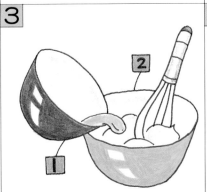

Stir in egg yolk mixture.

Add grated lemon rind and fold in sifted flour, cornstarch and baking powder.

160–170°C
14–15 minutes
Center rack

Shape into 4 cm long oblongs with pastry bag onto foil-lined cookie sheets. Sprinkle confectioners' sugar over cookies and bake in 160–170°C preheated oven for 14–15 minutes.

**For Charlottes:**

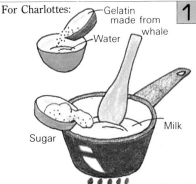

Soak gelatin in water. Combine milk and sugar in saucepan and dissolve sugar over low heat.

Stir in soaked gelatin. Remove from heat and add lightly beaten egg yolks. Leave to cool.

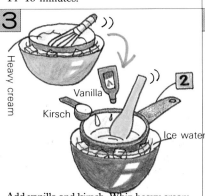

Add vanilla and kirsch. Whip heavy cream until peaks form. Add whipped cream to gelatin mixture.

Place ladyfingers along side of mold and pour into Bavarian cream. Refrigerate to chill.

Invert mold onto serving plate. Decorate with whipped cream and ribbon bow.

43

※ Liqueur, Kirsch: For Muslims, use only essence and don't use any liquor.

# Pretzels... *Typical German Cookies.*

*From dough into long thin rolls and twist into pretzel shapes on cookie sheets.*

**Ingredients (Makes 20 pretzels)**
For Dough A:
  120g   soft wheat flour;
  70g    butter;
  60g    sugar;
  1/2    egg;
  Few drops of vanilla oil.
Hard wheat flour for dusting.
For Glaze and Topping:
For B: Glacé icing (50g confectioners'
  sugar; 1 Ts water)
For C & D: Chopped almonds;
  Egg white; Chocolate.

**1** A

Sugar
Butter

Cream butter until light and fluffy, then add sugar one third at a time and mix well.

**2**

Vanilla
Egg

Stir in egg and vanilla oil.

**3**

Soft wheat flour

Fold in sifted flour with wooden spatula.

**4**

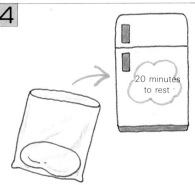

20 minutes to rest

Place in plastic bag and refrigerate for 20 minutes to rest.

**5**

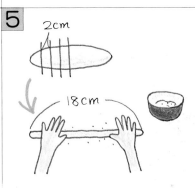

2cm

18cm

Divide dough into three and shape into rolls. Slice each roll with 2cm a part. Shape each piece into 18cm long thin roll.

**6**

A

Twist

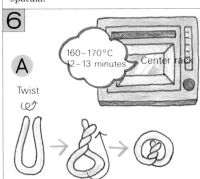

160–170°C
12–13 minutes   Center rack

Form each piece into U-shape on cookie sheet and twist as shown. Bake in 160–170°C preheated oven for 12–14 minutes.

Variation B:

Icing

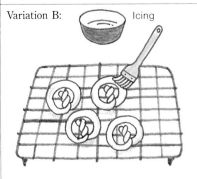

While pretzels are warm, brush icing.

Variation C:

**1**

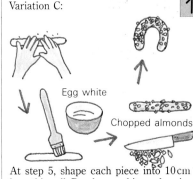

Egg white
Chopped almonds

At step 5, shape each piece into 10cm long thin roll. Brush egg white and sprinkle chopped almonds. Form into U-shape and bake.

**2**

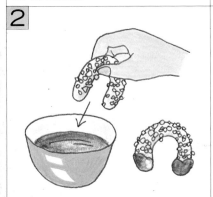

After cookies are cool, dip each end into chocolate.

Variation D:

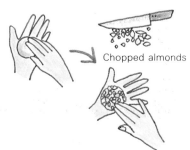

Chopped almonds

At step 5, shape each piece into rounds with hands, sprinkle chopped almonds and bake.

メモ

Note:

## How to serve cookies:

Most cookies contain much butter, so it is advisable to place lacy paper or fancy papernapkin onto serving plate, especially when you use silver or rattan plate.

# Ⓐ, Ⓑ Langues des Chats; Ⓒ, Ⓓ Cigars...

*Langue de Chat means "Tongue of Cat" and Cigar "Cigarette". They will melt in the mouth.*

## Ingredients (Makes 20 cookies)

For Batter:
- 60 g  soft wheat flour;
- 60 g  butter;
- 40 g  sugar;
- 1  egg white;
- Grated lemon rind;
- Meringue  (1 egg white and 10 g sugar.)

For Finishing:
- A:  Attach slivered almonds.
- B:  Shape over rolling pin.
- C:  Roll around a foil-covered pencil.
- D:  Dip ends into chocolate.

You may drop batter with spoon.

**1 A**

Cream butter until light and fluffy, then add sugar one half at a time and mix well.

**2**

Stir in lightly beaten egg white, one half at a time. Add grated lemon rind.

**3**

Fold in sifted flour with wooden spatula.

**4**

Beat egg white until stiff peaks form. Add sugar and continue to beat.

**5**

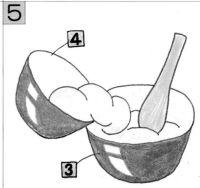

Fold meringue into flour mixture.

**6**

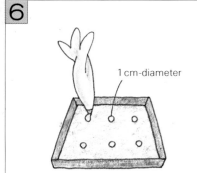

Form 1 cm-diameter rounds onto cookie sheets with pastry bag. Place sliced almonds on top of each cookie.

**7**

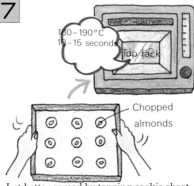

Let batter spread by tapping cookie sheet lightly. Bake in 180–190°C preheated oven for 10–15 seconds.

**8**

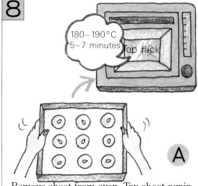

Remove sheet from oven. Tap sheet again to let batter spread and bake for 5–7 minutes.

**Variations B & C: B**

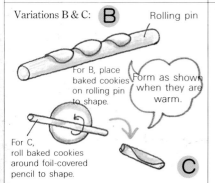

Shape 3 cm diameter rounds with pastry bag, bake in same manner and form as shown when they are warm.

**Variation D:**

Form thin rolls as for C and dip each end into chocolate. Let them dry placing on board.

**Note:**

## How to eat cookies:

Hold cookie with your hand and use paper napkin to get crumbs.
Use fork eating cake, cutting it into small piece.

# Let's have a cookie party

No one can resist to get together and enjoy chattering over coffee or tea and homemade cookies. It is a good way to get new friends as well as renew friendship. Why don't you invite your friends, neighbors or acquaintances to your home and spend a delightful afternoon over coffee, tea and cookies.

Bake two or three kinds of cookies, for example, Sablés, dropped butter cookies and nut cookies, and serve them on lovely plates. Prepare all the necessary things on a table as shown. Prepare coffee, tea and green tea, etc. It is advisable to prepare sandwiches and fruits. Please remember that your hospitality is the most important of all.